Saturn

Uranus

Neptune

Pluto

Human Space Exploration

Editor-in-chief: Paul A. Kobasa

Writer: Karen Ingebretsen

Editors: Jeff De La Rosa, Lisa Kwon, Maureen Liebenson,
Christine Sullivan

Research: Mike Barr, Jacqueline Jasek, Barbara Lightner,
Andy Roberts, Loranne Shields

Graphics and Design: Sandra Dyrlund, Charlene Epple,
Brenda Tropinski

Photos: Kathy Creech, Tom Evans

Permissions: Janet Peterson

Indexing: David Pofelski

Proofreading: Anne Dillon

Text processing: Curley Hunter, Gwendolyn Johnson

Pre-press and Manufacturing: Carma Fazio, Anne Fritzinger,
Steven Hueppchen, Madelyn Underwood

World Book, Inc.
233 N. Michigan Avenue
Chicago, IL 60601
U.S.A.

Library of Congress Cataloging-in-Publication Data

Human space exploration.
p. cm. -- (World Book's solar system &
space exploration library)
Includes bibliographical references and index.
ISBN 0-7166-9509-X
1. Manned space flight--Juvenile literature. 2. Outer
space--Exploration--Juvenile literature.
I. World Book, Inc.   II. Series.
TL793 .H79 2006
629.45--dc22
2005034771

ISBN (set) 0-7166-9500-6

Printed in the United States of America

1 2 3 4 5 6 7 8 09 08 07 06

**For information about other World Book publications,
visit our Web site at http://www.worldbook.com
or call 1-800-WORLDBK (967-5325).**

**For information about sales to schools and libraries,
call 1-800-975-3250 (United States);
1-800-837-5365 (Canada).**

Picture Acknowledgments: Front & Back Cover: NASA; Inside Front Cover: © John Gleason, Celestial
Images.

© Corbis/Bettmann 11; © Hulton Deutsch Collection/Corbis 27; © Richard T. Nowitz, Corbis 61; ESA/D.
Ducros 51; Esther C. Goddard 9; NASA 1, 3, 7, 15, 17, 19, 21, 23, 25, 27, 29, 31, 33, 35, 37, 39, 41, 43,
45, 49, 53, 55; NASA/John Frassanito and Associates 47; © Jeff Greenberg, Photo Edit 57; © Victor Habbick
Visions/Photo Researchers 59.

Illustrations: Inside Back Cover: WORLD BOOK illustration by Steve Karp; WORLD BOOK illustration by
Oxford Illustrators Limited 13.

Astronomers use different kinds of photos to learn about objects in space—such as planets. Many photos
show an object's natural color. Other photos use false colors. Some false-color images show types of light
the human eye cannot normally see. Others have colors that were changed to highlight important features.
When appropriate, the captions in this book state whether a photo uses natural or false color.

WORLD BOOK'S

SOLAR SYSTEM & SPACE EXPLORATION LIBRARY

Human Space Exploration

World Book, Inc.
a Scott Fetzer company
Chicago

Contents

HUMAN SPACE EXPLORATION

If a word is printed in **bold letters that look like this,** that word's meaning is given in the glossary on page 63.

Where Does Space Begin?

There is no clear boundary between the **atmosphere** of the Earth and outer space. The farther you go from Earth's surface, the thinner the air gets. But most scientists say that outer space begins about 60 miles (95 kilometers) above Earth.

Many countries agree that the **Karman Line,** an imaginary boundary about 62 miles (100 kilometers) above Earth's surface, is the start of outer space.

When humans decided to travel beyond Earth, they chose Earth's **moon** as the first place to visit. This made sense, because the moon is much closer to Earth than any of the **planets** in our **solar system.** Less fuel and time would be needed to reach the moon than other destinations. The moon is about 238,897 miles (384,467 kilometers) from Earth. By comparison, Venus—the planet closest to Earth— is about 23.7 million miles (about 38.2 million kilometers) away. Pluto is over 2.5 billion miles (over 4 billion kilometers) from Earth.

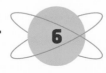

Earth's horizon shown against the blackness of space in a natural-color photo

When Did People First Explore Space?

In the 1930's, scientists began to build and test rockets that they hoped would one day be used for space travel. Starting around 1955, other scientists developed artificial **satellites** that were to be launched into space using rockets.

The Soviet Union (U.S.S.R.) was a powerful country that existed from 1922 to 1991. In 1957, the Soviet Union launched the first artificial satellite. This satellite, called Sputnik *(SPUHT nihk),* had no **astronauts** on board. Unpiloted satellites were a way of learning more about space before sending humans there. The Soviet Union was also the first to launch a **probe** to the surface of the **moon.** That probe, Luna 2, launched in 1959.

The first satellites that the United States launched successfully were Explorer 1 and Vanguard 1. They were launched in 1958. Vanguard 1 is still in orbit today. This satellite has sent a lot of information to Earth, including data that proved that Earth is slightly pear-shaped, not perfectly round. This information has helped map makers make more accurate world maps.

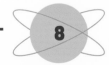

Scientists assist rocket pioneer Robert H. Goddard (left)

What Was the "Space Race"?

In the late 1950's and early 1960's, the United States and the Soviet Union were political rivals. Both countries were working on space exploration programs at that time. The launch of the **satellite** Sputnik—later called Sputnik 1—in 1957 surprised America, and U.S. leaders vowed to do whatever was needed to catch up. This was the start of the "space race."

Soon after, the National Aeronautics and Space Administration (NASA) was founded in the United States. This space agency gathered together researchers and laboratories and allowed people to work together toward the goal of space exploration. NASA was an important part of the eventual success of the American space program.

The space race faded by the 1970's, when both the United States and the Soviet Union began to pursue their independent goals in space. Today, many nations are working together on cooperative projects in space, including the International Space Station, or ISS (see page 50). Both Russia, which was once part of the Soviet Union, and the United States are involved in building the ISS.

The Soviet satellite Sputnik 1, resting in a stand before its launch

What Were the First Piloted Spacecraft Like?

The very first piloted spacecraft had room for only one person. That spacecraft was the Soviet Union's Vostok. The Vostok was designed to land with a parachute. The first type of piloted spacecraft designed by the United States—the Mercury spacecraft—was designed to land in the ocean.

As space programs continued, the **capsules** where the **astronauts** sit were made bigger so that two or more people could travel on a flight. These capsules were also able to carry more supplies so that astronauts could stay in space longer. The first spacecraft could stay in space for only about a day, but soon spacecraft could function for up to two weeks in space.

American spacecraft have sometimes been changed because of feedback from astronauts. For example, early astronauts asked that the window on board the spacecraft be made larger, and NASA did so. The escape **hatch** was also redesigned. After a tragic fire in 1967 on Apollo 1 in which three astronauts died, a new hatch was made that could be opened in just a few seconds, instead of the 90 seconds that were needed to open the old hatch.

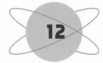

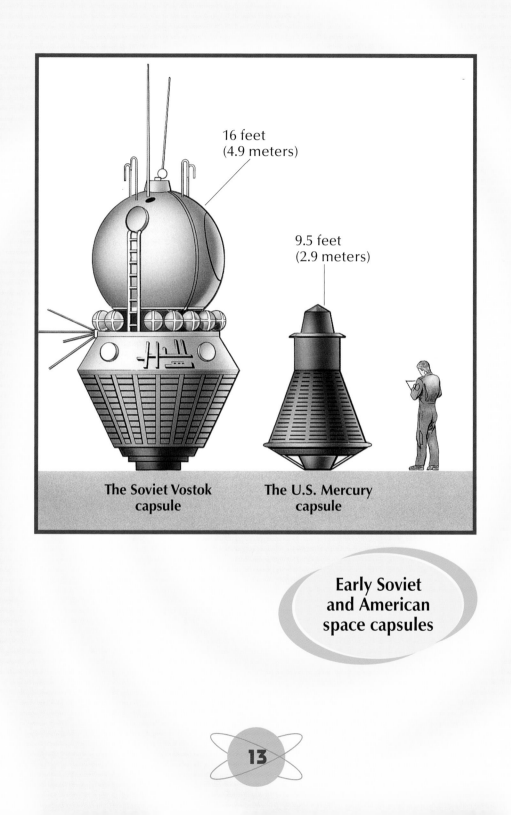

16 feet
(4.9 meters)

9.5 feet
(2.9 meters)

The Soviet Vostok
capsule

The U.S. Mercury
capsule

Early Soviet
and American
space capsules

What Gives a Spacecraft the Power for Liftoff?

Overcoming **gravity** is a spacecraft's biggest challenge. To overcome the force of gravity, a rocket called a **launch vehicle** is used. This rocket has a great deal of power and helps a spacecraft overcome gravity and reach space.

Rockets burn liquid or solid fuel. This fuel is combined with an oxidizer *(OK suh DY zuhr),* something that adds the **oxygen** needed to make the fuel burn in the airlessness of space. Rockets are made up of stages, or sections. Each stage falls away after it is used up, so that the rest of the spacecraft is lighter. That helps the spacecraft use less fuel and energy as it continues in space.

Sometimes rockets called **boosters** are attached to the launch vehicle. Boosters help especially heavy spacecraft overcome gravity.

The space shuttle
Discovery lifts off

Is Space Exploration Dangerous?

Yes, there are many dangers in space exploration. Tragic accidents have taken the lives of **astronauts** in both the United States and Soviet space programs.

Some of the risks of traveling or living in space are from things scientists know about and can protect against. Double hulls (the outer walls of a spacecraft) protect against damage from micrometeoroids (dust particles) and debris (space trash). Filters on the windows of a spacecraft protect against blinding **ultraviolet rays** from the sun. Heat shields and a thermal-control system keep people inside the craft safe from the extreme heat and cold of space.

Other risks are harder to predict. Spacecraft are complex vehicles, and it is not always possible to know how something may go wrong. When an explosion occurred on the Apollo 13 spacecraft in 1970, only the fast thinking of the crew in space and the NASA scientists on the ground allowed the spacecraft to return to Earth with the astronauts alive.

A U.S. naval crew recovers the damaged Apollo 13 spacecraft at sea

What Is Microgravity, and How Does It Affect Space Travel?

Most people have seen pictures of **astronauts** on board a spacecraft, floating in what is called "zero **gravity**" or "weightlessness." This condition is actually known as **microgravity,** and during space flights it has a major effect both on astronauts and on their spacecraft.

Microgravity affects the human body in many different ways. In the first few days of a mission, about half of all space travelers experience a "space sickness." Travelers feel disoriented—like they are always upside down, no matter which way they turn. They may become sick and may vomit. Medicines can help relieve the symptoms, and the condition usually goes away after a few days. Other effects on the body include a muscle weakness known as deconditioning.

Microgravity affects a spacecraft just as much as it does the astronauts. In a microgravity environment, fuel does not drain from tanks, so it must be squeezed out by high-pressure gas. Hot air does not rise in microgravity, so air does not circulate naturally, and fans must be used.

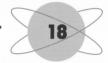

Candies (top) and
an astronaut (below) float
in microgravity

Who Was the First Person to Travel in Space?

A **cosmonaut** from the Soviet Union named Yuri Gagarin *(YOOR ee gah GAHR ihn)* was the first person to travel in space. He circled Earth on April 12, 1961, in a trip that lasted 1 hour and 48 minutes. After the flight, he returned safely to Earth.

The first American to travel in space was Alan B. Shepard, Jr. On May 5, 1961, he rocketed 117 miles (188 kilometers) into space and landed back on Earth 15 minutes later.

But even before humans first explored space, animals traveled on board spacecraft. An 11-pound dog named Laika *(LY kuh)* was the first space passenger. Laika flew aboard the Soviet craft Sputnik 2 in 1957. Other animal passengers included a chimpanzee named Ham, who made a 16-minute flight in a U.S. Mercury **capsule** in 1961. Over the years, space flights have also included bees, fish, frogs, mice, snails, and other animals.

Yuri Gagarin traveling
to the launch pad on
April 12, 1961

Who Was the First Person to Walk in Space? To Walk on the Moon?

Soviet **cosmonaut** Alexei Leonov *(uh lyih KSYAY lee OH nohf)* became the first person to step outside a spacecraft and float freely in space. This first spacewalk took place on March 18, 1965. Complications could have turned it into a fatal disaster. When he tried to go back inside the spacecraft, he learned that his spacesuit had inflated so much that at first he could not bend his body to enter the opening to the **airlock.** Finally he was able to reduce the pressure in his suit enough to get back on board Voshkod 2.

United States **astronaut** Neil A. Armstrong was the first person to walk on the surface of the **moon.** He took the first steps on this barren landscape on July 20, 1969, saying the now-famous words, "That's one small step for a man, one giant leap for mankind."

Neil Armstrong walking on the moon in 1969

Three still photos from a movie camera on Voshkod 2, showing Alexei Leonov outside the craft

What Did Astronauts Take from the Moon? Leave on the Moon?

During all six **moon** landings, U.S. Apollo **astronauts** collected rock and soil samples to take back to Earth for study. Altogether, astronauts gathered about 840 pounds (384 kilograms) of samples.

You can see moon rocks on display in the National Museum of Natural History in Washington, D.C., and in several other United States museums. A small number of rocks have been given to other countries as goodwill gifts. Most of the material returned by the Apollo missions is stored in NASA vaults.

As for what has been left on the moon, astronauts Neil A. Armstrong and Buzz Aldrin planted a U.S. flag on the moon during their first moonwalk, on July 20, 1969. In addition to the flag, they also left a plaque on the moon, shown at right.

And, of course, astronauts left their footprints on the moon as well. Since there is no wind or water on the moon to disturb them, the footprints should last for millions of years.

A moon rock (left), and a flag and plaque left on the moon by American astronauts

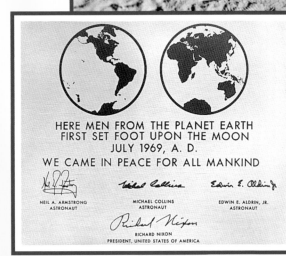

HERE MEN FROM THE PLANET EARTH
FIRST SET FOOT UPON THE MOON
JULY 1969, A. D.
WE CAME IN PEACE FOR ALL MANKIND

NEIL A. ARMSTRONG
ASTRONAUT

MICHAEL COLLINS
ASTRONAUT

EDWIN E. ALDRIN, JR.
ASTRONAUT

RICHARD NIXON
PRESIDENT, UNITED STATES OF AMERICA

Who Were Some Notable Astronauts?

In addition to astronauts already discussed, notable people who traveled in space include Valentina Tereshkova *(VAH lehn TEE nah teh rehsh KAW vah)*. Tereshkova, a Soviet **cosmonaut,** was the first woman in space. She made the flight in Vostok 6 in June 1963. The first U.S. woman in space was Sally K. Ride, who, along with four other **astronauts,** made a six-day flight on the space shuttle Challenger in June 1983.

Also aboard Challenger, in August 1983, Guion S. Bluford, Jr., became the first African American to go into space. In September 1992, on the space shuttle Endeavour, Mae C. Jemison became the first African American woman to do so.

The youngest astronaut to travel in space was Soviet cosmonaut Gherman Titov *(GUR men TEE tohf)*. He was 25 years old when he piloted Vostok 2 in August 1961. The oldest was retired astronaut John H. Glenn, who, in 1998, flew aboard the space shuttle Discovery. Glenn was 77 years old at that time.

The first Canadian in space was Marc Garneau, on the space shuttle Challenger in 1984.

Valentina Tereshkova (top),
John Glenn (middle), and
Guion Bluford, Jr. (bottom)

What Kinds of Experiments Have Been Carried Out in Space?

Many space experiments have been designed to study the effects of **microgravity** on animals, plants, and people. Spacelab, a reusable laboratory, traveled in the cargo bay of NASA's space shuttle on various missions between 1983 and 1997. In Spacelab, scientists researched many different fields of science, including microgravity and the life sciences.

Sometimes students have been allowed to suggest experiments. For example, in 1973, **astronauts** on Skylab, the first United States space station, conducted an experiment that a high-school student suggested. The student wanted to know if spiders could spin webs in microgravity. The spiders chosen needed some time to adjust to near-weightlessness, but they were able to spin webs. The silk was finer and less even, however, than what they had spun on Earth.

A spider in a web spun in microgravity (right) and a scientist on the space shuttle experiments with bees (below)

What Is the Space Shuttle Like?

The space shuttle system is made up of three parts: (1) an **orbiter,** (2) an external fuel tank, and (3) two solid rocket **boosters.** The nose (front) of the orbiter houses the crew cabin. As many as seven **astronauts** typically live and work in the cabin. From the **flight deck** at the front of the orbiter, the pilot can look through the front and side windows. The middeck, located under the flight deck, contains more seats, equipment lockers, sleeping facilities, and a small toilet compartment. The "kitchen" on the space shuttle includes hot- and cold-water dispensers, an oven, serving trays for food, and a water heater, but no freezer or refrigerator. The payload bay is the area that holds the cargo, or goods, hauled by the shuttle. The tail of the orbiter houses the engines.

The space shuttle was the first reusable spacecraft. To be reused, the shuttle had to land on solid ground, not water, so it was designed to take off like a rocket but land like an airplane. The shuttle's engines are designed to be reusable for many missions. It also has a heat shield that can withstand many reentries into Earth's atmosphere.

The space shuttle Discovery is readied for launch

Rocket booster

Fuel tank

Rocket booster

Orbiter

What's for Dinner in Space?

The food served on a spacecraft has come a long way since the Mercury **astronauts** dined in space. Those early astronauts had to squeeze their semiliquid foods (said to be less than tasty) out of aluminum tubes similar to toothpaste tubes.

Today, astronauts have many choices of things to eat, including macaroni and cheese, beef, peanut butter and jelly, chicken soup, brownies, apples, carrot sticks, and nuts. Some modern meals in space are ready-to-eat. The astronauts have to add water to other foods. Meals can be heated in an oven on board.

All drinks, even coffee and cocoa, are served in a pouch with a straw or in a squeeze bottle. That's because in **microgravity,** if you tip a cup, the liquid will not move toward your mouth.

In space, astronauts can eat upside down, or at least upside down in relation to the spacecraft. That's because in microgravity there is no true "up" or "down."

A meal shared on the
International Space
Station

How Do Astronauts Handle Personal Hygiene ?

Even in space, you cannot get out of keeping clean. It's true that there is no shower, bathtub, or sink on the space shuttle, since room and water are limited. But shuttle **astronauts** can "bathe" by rubbing alcohol wipes or wet washcloths over their bodies. They wash their hair with rinseless shampoos. They brush their teeth with a regular toothbrush and toothpaste, and then spit into a tissue.

On the International Space Station (ISS), crew members wash with wet towels. Perhaps in the future, a shower will be installed as well. NASA's Skylab space station had a shower. When astronauts washed in it, water and soap stuck to their skin because of **microgravity.** The water had to be "vacuumed off" after they had finished bathing.

Except when they are wearing pressure suits, astronauts on the space shuttle and the ISS use toilets that flush with air, not water. The toilets basically work like vacuum cleaners, with fans that suck air and waste into a storage tank. Astronauts must clamp themselves to the seat while using the toilet, to keep from floating away.

An astronaut in the
shower on Skylab

What Do Astronauts Wear on a Space Mission?

Crews on the space shuttle wear special suits for launch and reentry and for **extravehicular activity (EVA),** or work outside of the spacecraft. Launch and Entry Suits (LES) protect against fire and keep pressure around the **astronauts'** bodies in case the spacecraft's pressurization systems fail. Space suits used for EVA function like a self-contained spacecraft to keep the astronaut safe.

On the International Space Station, and inside the shuttle after launch and before reentry, astronauts wear ordinary shorts or pants, a short- or long-sleeved shirt, and socks. The pants and shorts have plenty of pockets with Velcro closings to secure objects that would otherwise float away.

Crews on the shuttle get a change of clothes for each day of the mission. But on the ISS, where there is no washing machine, astronauts do not change clothes as often as we do on Earth. They change their work shirts and pants or shorts about once every 10 days. When clothing is dirty and cannot be worn any more, it is usually placed in a returning resupply vehicle that burns up when the vehicle reenters Earth's atmosphere.

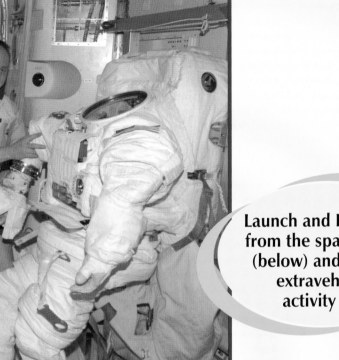

Launch and Entry Suits from the space shuttle (below) and suits for extravehicular activity (left)

Do You Get Your Own Bedroom in Space?

Well, it depends on which spacecraft you are traveling in. On the International Space Station there are small crew cabins, just big enough for one person. Each cabin has a sleeping bag and a window that looks out into space.

On the shuttle, there are no individual rooms for each crew member. Because of **microgravity,** shuttle **astronauts** could drift around the spacecraft as they slept. But most prefer to use bunk beds or sleeping bags that can be clipped to walls, the ceiling, or a seat. Or, they may decide to sleep strapped into the commander's or pilot's seats. All of these sleep choices prevent astronauts from bumping into each other or into equipment and walls that would wake or injure them. In microgravity, sleeping bags can be attached in any position that is practical. Since there is no "up" in space, the astronauts can sleep just as comfortably positioned vertically as they can horizontally.

On the shuttle, astronauts may wear sleeping masks at bedtime to block the sunlight that streams in the windows at times during **orbit.**

Astronauts strapped in and wearing blindfolds to sleep

What Is the Shuttle Used For?

Space shuttles carry artificial **satellites,** space **probes,** and other heavy loads into **orbit** around Earth. In addition to launch operations where the shuttle takes things into space, a shuttle can retrieve artificial satellites that need repair. **Astronauts** aboard the shuttle can fix a satellite and then return it to orbit. Shuttle crews can also conduct many kinds of scientific experiments and observations.

In 1993, a crew from the shuttle Endeavour repaired the orbiting Hubble Space Telescope. The astronauts installed equipment that canceled out the effect of an error in the telescope's main mirror. This enabled the telescope to capture and send images in detail never seen before. In its first 15 years, the telescope took three-quarters of a million photos.

Shuttles also are used to take crews and cargo to and from the International Space Station. The shuttle Endeavour carried Unity, the second major section of the space station, into orbit in 1998. In 2005, the shuttle Discovery delivered several tons of supplies and equipment to the station.

Astronauts from the shuttle Endeavour repair the Hubble Space Telescope

How Do Astronauts Train for Shuttle Missions?

NASA has developed many tools to help **astronauts** train for shuttle missions. Many of these tools allow the crews to practice handling unexpected problems, so that if these problems do arise during a mission, the crew is prepared to deal with them safely.

For training in launch (taking off), ascent (going up), reentry (entering Earth's atmosphere), and landing, a shuttle crew uses a device called the motion-based simulator. It has a copy of the space shuttle flight deck. The simulator rocks, rolls, moves side-to-side, and vibrates just like the real shuttle orbiter. This allows the crew to practice handling different equipment problems and emergency landings. Astronauts also practice in a fixed-base simulator. It has a replica of the flight deck and most of the middeck. Here, a crew trains for most of the tasks to be performed while in **orbit.**

To train for **extravehicular activity,** or work outside a vehicle in space, astronauts use the Neutral Buoyancy Laboratory. One of the largest indoor pools in the world, the laboratory is used to simulate the weightless condition that the crew will experience during space flight.

An astronaut trains in the Neutral Buoyancy Laboratory

Who Is In Charge of the Shuttle on the Ground?

Ground preparations for a mission may begin weeks or months before the launch date. Launch Control at the Kennedy Space Center in Florida is in charge of the shuttle all through preparation, until the message "tower clear" is announced. This message is broadcast a few seconds into the launch. It means that the shuttle has cleared the launch tower—the tower that holds and supports the craft in an upright position before take off—and has successfully launched. Then, Mission Control at the Johnson Space Center in Houston, Texas, takes over. Mission Control remains in charge until the wheels stop when the **orbiter** has landed back on Earth.

Actually, the word "control" in the titles of both these groups is a little misleading. If everything is working as it should, nobody—not even the astronauts on board—controls the shuttle during launch or reentry. The shuttle uses its own computers to fly into and out of **orbit.** Launch Control, Mission Control, and the **astronauts** watch their monitors, and these professionals step in if something is not working correctly.

Mission Control at the
Johnson Space Center

When Will the Space Shuttle Retire?

The space shuttle has been a step forward in the space program because it is mostly reusable. That was not true of any spacecraft built before the shuttle. Even though the shuttle is used over and over, shuttle missions are very expensive to fly—some estimates are one billion dollars per mission—and the fleet of **orbiters** is aging.

Further, safety concerns have continued to plague the space shuttle. The first space shuttle mission flew in 1981. Since that time, two shuttles missions have ended in disaster. In 1986, the shuttle Challenger broke apart shortly after launch and all seven astronauts aboard were killed. In 2003, the space shuttle Columbia broke apart as it reentered Earth's atmosphere. All seven crew members died in this disaster as well.

The age of the shuttle program, the shuttle's expense, and its safety record have led experts to call for a new spacecraft to replace the shuttle. In recent years, several organizations have been working to develop this replacement craft.

An artist's drawing of a new spacecraft proposed by NASA to replace the space shuttle

What Is a Space Station?

A space station is a place where people can live and work in space for long periods. One major reason to have a space station is that the equipment only has to be carried into space one time. Once it is in space, many **astronauts** from one or more countries can reuse it.

A space station **orbits** Earth, usually at about 200 to 300 miles (300 to 480 kilometers) above Earth's surface. A space station may serve as an observatory, laboratory, factory, workshop, warehouse, and fuel depot for refueling spacecraft.

Space stations are much larger than piloted spacecraft, so they provide more comforts. Piloted spacecraft may transport people between Earth and the space station. Unpiloted spacecraft may supply the station with food, water, equipment, and even deliver the mail.

The Soviet Union's Salyut 1, launched in 1971, was the first space station. It hosted a 23-day mission. Skylab, the first United States space station, was in orbit from 1973 through 1979. Mir was the longest-lived station, in orbit from 1986 to 2001. The Soviet Union launched Mir, and Russia later took it over.

The Mir
space station

What Is the International Space Station?

The International Space Station is a large, inhabited Earth **satellite** being built in space. The space station is being built in **modules,** or pieces. The first module, Zarya, was built and launched by Russia in 1998. The second, Unity, was built and launched by the United States later in 1998. As modules arrive in space, they are joined to the existing modules. When complete, the space station will consist of about eight main modules.

What is most unusual about the station is that it is a truly international station. More than 15 nations, including the United States, Canada, and Russia, are partners in the project. The joining of the Zarya and Unity modules in space symbolized the start of a new era in cooperation between nations in space exploration. This cooperation was seen again when safety concerns caused NASA to ground the U.S. shuttle fleet for a time from 2003 to 2005. When that happened, the Russian Soyuz missions took charge of supplying the station and transporting **astronauts.** Every six months, Russia flies a new Soyuz spacecraft to the station to be used as an escape vehicle in case of a life-threatening emergency.

An artist's conception
of the completed
International Space
Station

What Have We Learned So Far on the International Space Station?

Ever since the first piloted space flights, scientists have studied the effects of space exposure and **microgravity** on the human body. **Astronauts** on the International Space Station continue this research, which is even more important now that people can spend months at a time in space. What we learn today may one day be used on ultralong flights.

Astronauts on the space station also are carrying out experiments with construction materials. They expose hundreds of possible future space construction materials to the environment of space. Then, samples are returned to Earth and studied. NASA hopes the results help to build stronger, more durable spacecraft.

Astronauts are not the only people conducting research from the space station. A NASA program called Earth Knowledge Acquired by Middle School Students (EarthKAM) allows thousands of middle school students to photograph and study Earth, using a digital camera mounted on the International Space Station.

An astronaut performs a microgravity experiment on the International Space Station

What Things Do We Use Today That Were Created for the Space Program?

Technology developed for NASA missions has been used in everyday products in many fields, including health and medicine, transportation, recreation, computer technology, and public safety.

NASA developed the materials and technologies that are used in smoke detectors, ear thermometers, TV satellite dishes, joystick controllers for video games, transparent braces for teeth, and football helmets that absorb shocks three times as well as old helmets. Cordless tools also were originally developed by NASA to help Apollo astronauts drill for moon samples.

An astronaut
working with a cordless
power tool

How Can Kids Get Involved in Space Exploration?

There are many ways that young people can get involved in space exploration. You can play a part from your home with a computer and Internet connection.

Boy Scout and Girl Scout organizations offer space-exploration achievement badges. To earn the badges, kids learn about the history of space travel, visit a place related to air travel, or even build and launch model rockets.

NASA sponsors many programs for schools. In the "Send Your Art to Space" program, kids were invited to submit a piece of art that represented their school. That art was then sent to the International Space Station on a compact disc.

With a personal computer, you can tune into NASA Direct—live webcasts leading up to every shuttle launch. These webcasts feature scientists, engineers, NASA managers, and **astronauts.** And during shuttle missions you can watch NASA TV on the Internet, with start-to-finish coverage from Mission Control.

A Cub Scout at the
NASA Space Center.

Where Do I Sign Up?

Since the first piloted space flight, fewer than 1,000 people have flown in space. Even if someone qualified as an **astronaut** and were hired, there is no guarantee he or she would be on a mission anytime soon. What other ways might there be to experience space travel and tourism in the future?

A few wealthy civilians have paid to travel to the International Space Station (ISS) aboard Russian spacecraft. Space Adventures, the private company that arranged the trips, also offers **microgravity** training, simulated spacewalk training, simulator training on the Soviet Soyuz spacecraft, and other programs.

The private British company Virgin Galactic is taking deposits for brief flights into space on the VSS Enterprise. The VSS Enterprise is a commercial spacecraft the company hopes to start flying within several years.

Several other companies have developed plans for space hotels, including hotels on the moon. Who knows what will be next in space tourism? After all, not even the sky is the limit!

An artist's conception of a hotel in space

So You Want to Become a Space Explorer?

To become a NASA **astronaut,** you must have at least a bachelor's degree in engineering, science, or math. An advanced degree is desirable. You also need to have completed three years of related experience after graduation. Pilot astronauts must have at least 1,000 hours of experience in jet aircraft. Competition is extremely stiff. Usually, over 4,000 people apply for about 20 openings every two years.

Supporting the astronauts on every mission are many thousands of other workers, in jobs ranging from research pilots to microbiologists. Requirements for these vital jobs vary, depending on the job.

To experience a simulated space mission, some kids visit a Challenger Learning Center. These centers offer scale models of mission control and an orbiting space station.

And for sheer fun, nothing beats space camp. At space camps in the United States, Canada, and Europe, kids may meet astronauts, try out motion and microgravity simulators, and design space robots.

Sitting in the cockpit of a shuttle at space camp

FUN FACTS About HUMAN SPACE EXPLORATION

★ In October 2003, China became the third nation to independently launch a person into space. Chinese **astronaut** Yang Liwei orbited Earth aboard a Shenzhou craft for 21 hours before landing safely.

★ Two identical Skylabs were built. One was launched and the other was kept as a backup. The backup is on display at the National Air and Space Museum in Washington, D.C.

★ "Escape velocity" is the speed necessary to break free of Earth's **gravity.**

★ Belka and Strelka were dogs that **orbited** Earth aboard Sputnik 5 (August 1960) and returned safely to Earth. Strelka later gave birth to puppies; one of the pups was given to the daughter of President John F. Kennedy as a gift from the Soviet Union.

★ More than 15 nations are taking part in building the International Space Station (ISS), including the United States, Canada, Japan, Russia, Belgium, Denmark, France, Germany, Italy, the Netherlands, Norway, Spain, Sweden, Switzerland and the United Kingdom. In addition, Brazil and Italy have signed on as payload participants, or specialists on scientific experiments aboard spacecraft.

Glossary

airlock On a spacecraft, the chamber between the outer door that leads to space and the door leading to the inside of the spacecraft.

astronaut A pilot or member of the crew of a spacecraft.

atmosphere The mass of gases that surrounds a planet.

booster A rocket sometimes attached to a launch vehicle to provide extra power.

capsule A section of a spacecraft that can be used or ejected as a unit.

cosmonaut A Russian astronaut.

extravehicular activity (EVA) Work or other activity outside of a spacecraft.

flight deck The uppermost compartment of the cabin in a space shuttle, which contains the controls for the shuttle's guidance and navigation.

gravity The effect of a force of attraction that acts between all objects because of their mass (that is, the amount of matter the objects have).

hatch A door or opening on a spacecraft that can be sealed.

Karman Line An altitude of about 62 miles (100 kilometers) above Earth's surface (from sea level). This height has become an international boundary marking the beginning of outer space.

launch vehicle A rocket that carries a satellite or spacecraft into space.

microgravity A condition of very low gravity, especially approaching weightlessness.

module A piece or section of a spacecraft; often a module can be used as one unit.

moon A smaller body that orbits a planet.

orbit The path that a smaller body takes around a larger body, for instance, the path that a planet takes around the sun. Also, to travel in an orbit.

orbiter In the space shuttle, a winged craft that looks like an airplane and which holds the cabin where the astronauts are.

oxygen A nonmetallic chemical element.

planet A large, round body in space that orbits a star and shines with light reflected from that star.

probe An unpiloted device sent to explore space. Most probes send data (information) from space.

satellite A natural satellite is an object that orbits a planet or asteroid. An artificial satellite is a manufactured object launched by rocket into an orbit around Earth or another body in space. Artificial satellites are used to send weather or other scientific information back to Earth.

solar system A group of bodies in space made up of a star and the planets and other objects orbiting around the star.

ultraviolet rays An invisible form of light. The sun is the major natural source of ultraviolet rays on Earth.

Index

For more information about human space exploration, try these resources:

Frontiers of Space Exploration, 2nd ed., by Roger D. Launius, Greenwood Press, 2004

Escape from Earth: Voyages Through Time, by Peter Ackroyd, Dorling Kindersley, 2005

Aiming for the Stars: The Dreamers and Doers of the Space Age, by Tom D. Crouch, Smithsonian Books, 2000

http://curious.astro.cornell.edu/space.php

http://edspace.nasa.gov/

http://science.ksc.nasa.gov/history/history.html

http://www.bbc.co.uk/science/space/exploration/missiontimeline/